Visit the Library's On-line Catalog at:
http://www.zionsville.lib.in.us

Call the Library for information on access
if Internet is not available to you.
(317) 873-3149

On-line magazine index with full text at:
http://www.inspire-indiana.net

cool collectibles

BUTTERFLIES

Ned Simonson

HIGH
interest
books

A Division of Grolier Publishing
New York / London / Hong Kong / Sydney
Danbury, Connecticut

To my mom

Book Design: Michael DeLisio
Contributing Editor: Jennifer Ceaser

Photo Credits: Cover, p. 35 © FPG; p. 5, 6, 16, 32, © Superstock; p. 9, 19, 20, 25, 36, 39 © Peter Arnold; p. 12 © International Stock; p. 15, 23, 40 © KAC; p. 26, 30 © David Liebman

Visit Children's Press on the Internet at:
http://publishing.grolier.com

Library of Congress Cataloging-in-Publication Data

Simonson, Ned.
  Butterflies / by Ned Simonson.
    p. cm. – (Cool collectibles)
  Includes bibliographical references and index.
  Summary: Provides general information about butterflies and descriptions of different types, as well as explaining how to observe these creatures and how to raise a butterfly from a caterpillar.
  ISBN 0-516-23328-9 (lib. bdg.) – ISBN 0-516-23528-1 (pbk.)
  1. Butterflies—Juvenile literature. 2. Butterfly watching—Juvenile literature. 3. Butterfly gardening—Juvenile literature. [1. Butterflies. 2.Butterfly watching. 3. Butterfly gardening.] I. Title. II. Series.

QL544.2.S52 2000
595.78'9—dc21

                                                                    00-024360

CONTENTS

Introduction

Butterflies are some of Earth's most beautiful insects. They come in all shapes, sizes, and colors. Butterflies can be found almost anywhere in the world: from the Arctic to city parks to tropical rain forests.

Butterfly scientists, called lepidopterists, have studied and named butterflies for hundreds of years. Lepidopterists have discovered about twenty thousand species of butterflies. They find out about new butterfly species all the time.

Rather than killing and collecting these beautiful insects, people have become butterfly watchers. All over the world, people have made it their hobby to watch and study butterflies.

Watching butterflies can be hard work. It takes a sharp eye and a lot of patience and practice. Butterflies are not always easy to see. Many

Butterflies can be all different sizes, shapes, and colors.

butterflies have coloring that helps them to stay camouflaged (blended into their environment).

Anyone up to the challenge will enjoy the rewards of watching these wonderful creatures. So, are you ready to become a butterfly watcher?

What is a Butterfly?

A butterfly is a part of a large group of insects known as *Lepidoptera*. The name comes from two Greek words: *lepido*, meaning scale, and *ptera*, meaning wing. So, a butterfly is an insect with scales and wings. The butterfly doesn't actually have what we think of as scales. The wings of a butterfly are easy to see, but you must look very closely to see the insect's scales.

SCALES

Butterflies' bodies and colorful wings are covered with thousands of tiny hairs, called scales. The complex designs of a butterfly's wings are produced by thousands of scales. Each scale has a single color. The scales form patterns by overlapping one another like shingles on a roof.

A butterfly's wings are made up of thousands of scales that form beautiful patterns.

WING COLOR

A butterfly's wing color serves many purposes.

❀ The colors help a butterfly to camouflage itself in its environment. Camouflage helps to protect these delicate insects from birds, bigger insects, and other predators.

❀ Wing color helps male and female butterflies to recognize each other as the same species, so they can mate.

❀ Bright colors warn predators that a certain butterfly may taste bad. Bad-tasting butterflies include the Monarch and the Pipevine Swallowtail.

❀ Dark colors on the wings help the butterfly to soak up warmth from the sun. This warmth gives the insect energy to fly or to keep its body warm during cooler seasons.

PARTS OF A BUTTERFLY

As do other insects, butterflies have six legs and three main body parts. They have a head, a thorax (chest), and an abdomen (tail end). A pair of antennae is used as feelers. A butterfly uses its feet to taste and smell. It breathes through its stomach. It has a mouth that is actually a long tongue, called a proboscis. A butterfly's eyes allow it to see in all directions. Its eyes also are sensitive to color. Butterflies need to be able to recognize color to know on which plants to feed.

WHAT BUTTERFLIES EAT

Most insects chew their food with mandibles (jaws). Butterflies, however, stick to a liquid-only diet of nectar, sap, or the pulp of rotting fruit. A butterfly sucks up nectar through its tongue, which works like a straw. Some butterflies have tongues that are one and a half times as long as their bodies. This long

A butterfly has a very long tongue.

9

tongue allows the butterfly to reach deep into flowers for a drink.

FROM CATERPILLAR TO BUTTERFLY

Every butterfly starts life as an egg. It takes three to six days for the egg to hatch. The egg hatches to produce a caterpillar. The caterpillar's main purpose is to eat. Leaves and flowers are its usual food. Then, as it fattens up, the caterpillar molts (sheds its old skin). It does this

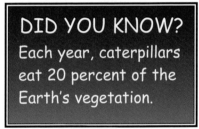

DID YOU KNOW?
Each year, caterpillars eat 20 percent of the Earth's vegetation.

many times, increasing up to several thousand times in size over two weeks. In fact, if a new-born human baby were to eat and grow as fast as a caterpillar does, in six weeks it would be the size of a double-decker bus!

Fat, full, and ready to rest, the caterpillar then spins a cocoon. Inside the cocoon, the caterpillar turns into a pupa, or chrysalis. In about two weeks, the insect will become a fully formed butterfly.

Butterfly or Moth?

There are many differences between butterflies and moths. Here are the most common ones:

❀ Most butterflies are diurnal (active during the day). Moths are nocturnal, which means that they usually only come out at night.

❀ While resting, a butterfly holds its wings together above its back. A moth holds its wings horizontally.

❀ Butterfly antennae are thick at the tips. Moth antennae are usually feathered at the tips.

Butterfly Watching

Butterfly watching can be rewarding in many ways. It can be a science, a hobby, or simply a fun way to spend the day outdoors. But first you need to find butterflies! Here are some tips for knowing where and when to look for them.

WHEN TO LOOK

Butterflies prefer warm weather. You'll see most butterflies on sunny days. Normally, butterflies fly between 9:00 A.M. and 4:00 P.M. The best time of the year to look for butterflies is from late spring through early fall.

WHERE TO LOOK

Most butterflies prefer open spaces with lots of native plants. A native plant is a plant that grows

This girl finds a butterfly in an open field. She uses a special net to catch the butterfly without harming it.

13

naturally in a particular region. Good places to start your search are sunny country roads, national parks, wildlife areas, meadows, and fields. Damp areas near streams and marshes also can be rich in butterflies.

The best time to see butterflies is when they stop to eat. A good place to start looking is among a group of colorful flowers in full bloom. Also, many butterfly species feed on the ground. They lick wet rocks and drink the juice out of fallen fruit. So be sure to watch your step when you are looking for butterflies.

If you don't live near a national park or large wildlife area, visit your local city or county park. Many parks plant butterfly gardens to attract butterflies in the summer. You also may want to visit a zoo or natural history museum. These institutions often have butterfly houses, called conservatories. You'll be able to walk around as hundreds of exotic butterflies flutter all around you.

At some national parks, you can walk through areas where there are hundreds of butterflies.

HOW TO WATCH A BUTTERFLY

When a butterfly stops to drink from a flower, most likely you will want to get a closer look. Approach the insect as quietly and as carefully as you can. Butterflies are very sensitive to movement, and you don't want to scare them away.

BUTTERFLY-WATCHING TOOLS

To watch butterflies in the wild, you will want to be prepared. There are some useful tools that will help you to get the most out of your butterfly-watching experience.

A camera with a zoom lens is a great way to capture butterflies on film.

Binoculars

Bring along a good pair of binoculars.A pair with the closest possible focusing distance is recommended. Look for binoculars that are powered for 12 feet (about 3.5 meters) or less.

Magnifying Glass

The best way to see butterflies up close is with a magnifying glass. Again, you will want to approach the insects very quietly. Don't hold the glass over the butterfly for longer than 30 seconds. Otherwise, you will concentrate the sun's rays on the insect and may accidentally harm it.

Guidebook

To get you started, we've identified a few of the more popular butterflies you can expect to see. (See Chapter 3.) There are thousands of different kinds of butterflies, and a guidebook can help you to recognize a particular species.

Camera

The most environmentally friendly way to capture a butterfly is by photographing it. So bring along a camera. If your camera has a zoom lens, you can take wonderful close-up pictures. Keep your butterfly "collection" in a photo album.

Notebook

Part of the fun of butterfly watching is keeping track of all the types of butterflies you have seen. Keep notes about each species that you see, and when and where you saw it. Remember, new butterfly species are being discovered all the time. Who knows? Maybe you'll make an amazing scientific discovery!

Tongs

You may want to get a closer look at a rare species. A pair of tongs is a good way to pick up a butterfly to examine it more closely. Tongs used for handling postage stamps work very well. Always handle a butterfly gently. Never touch their wings with your hands. Their wings are extremely fragile and can be easily damaged.

Net

You can buy a butterfly net at most larger pet stores. To catch a butterfly, you will need to swing the net quickly . Twist the net's handle so that the insect is in the tip of the net. Keep the butterfly in the tip by squeezing the net closed just above it. Place a container over the opening and allow the insect to crawl into it. Put the lid on the container.

This man uses a net with a long pole attached to catch butterflies high up in the trees.

Container

A container will come in handy when you want to show off a special butterfly to your friends. Buy a container with breathing holes or poke small holes in the top of a plastic container. The butterfly can be easily passed around in a small group and then released.

Types of Butterflies

There are hundreds of ways to identify species of butterflies. That's because butterflies come in all different sizes, shapes, and colors. In the United States and Canada alone, there are more than 750 different species of butterflies! To be a good butterfly watcher, you'll need to know how to spot the differences between these species. You can start by studying some of the most common butterflies in North America.

TIGER SWALLOWTAIL

A large and colorful butterfly, the Tiger Swallowtail gets its name from the black, tiger-like stripes found on its yellow wings. Females have patches of blue on their hindwings. This butterfly has hindwings (back wings) that are

The Tiger Swallowtail gets its name from the tigerlike pattern on its wings.

shaped like tails. Its wingspan (the distance between the tips of its wings) is 3½ to 6½ inches (9 to 16.5 cm). Tiger Swallowtails spend most of their time in the air. They usually only come to the ground to feed or lay eggs.

Great Spangled Fritillary

This is one of the world's largest butterflies, measuring 2¼ to 3 inches (5 to 7.5 cm). Its forewings (front wings) are ribbed, with

DID YOU KNOW?

The life span of a Spring Azure butterfly is just four days, but the Mourning Cloak can live for up to eleven months. Most butterflies live for only two weeks.

black spots. It has silver patches on its hindwings. Fritillaries spend most of their time in the air, flying around and feeding. July is the best month to spot these quick flyers.

Painted Lady

This butterfly is found almost everywhere in the world. It has a wing pattern of orange and black, speckled with white spots. This pattern makes

The Great Spangled Fritillary is one of the largest
butterflies in the world.

the Painted Lady one of the easiest species to
recognize. It has slight ribbing on its hindwings.
Also known as the Cosmopolitan butterfly, it
ranges from 2 to 2½ inches (5 to 6 cm) in size.

Buckeye

This popular species of butterfly gets its name
from the spots found on its wings. Buckeyes are
mostly brown with orange bands on their
forewings. Their wingspan reaches 2 to 2½
inches (5 to 6 cm).

23

Snout Butterfly

Guess how this butterfly got its name? Because of its odd nose, you may think that this butterfly would be easy to spot. Yet it's very small, only 1 to 1½ inches (2 to 4 cm), and it flies very fast.

Mourning Cloak

This species has a dark maroon upperside, and black-ringed blue spots running along the edge of its wings. The yellow border of the wings gives an unusual speckled effect. Also known as the Camberwell Beauty, this butterfly ranges from 2½ to 3¼ inches (6 to 8 cm) in length.

Butterfly Beliefs

For thousands of years, la mariposa (the butterfly) has played an active role in Mexican culture. Ancient Mayan Indians wore butterfly-shaped nose rings. Butterflies also were carved into temples and statues as decoration.

In modern-day Mexico, certain beliefs and superstitions are based on butterfly sightings. For example, some people believe that, when a black butterfly stops at your door, death is close by.

The Mourning Cloak has a unique yellow border on its wings.

4

Raising a Butterfly

One of the most rewarding ways to watch butterflies is to grow them from eggs. To see the change from egg to butterfly is to watch one of nature's most remarkable events. You can raise rare butterfly species or common species that are native to your area.

GROW YOUR OWN BUTTERFLY

We'll use a Monarch butterfly as our example. The Monarch is very common and easy to find.

❁ Locate a caterpillar. Because Monarch butterfly caterpillars eat milkweed, the best place to look is in a milkweed patch. These caterpillars have bright stripes across their bodies. They are easiest to find during the spring and early summer.

A Monarch caterpillar has bright stripes along its body.

❁ Try to avoid handling caterpillars. If you must, move them with a paintbrush. (Many caterpillar species have stinging hairs and should be handled carefully.)

❁ Place the caterpillar in a clear, open container with leaves on the bottom. Choose a container that has plenty of room for your caterpillar to grow. Jelly jars, plastic shoeboxes, or old fish tanks work well.

❁ Place paper towels at the bottom of the container. The paper towels will help to absorb moisture. This will prevent the leaves from growing mold. Cover the container with a fabric that is breathable, such as netting, nylon, or cheesecloth. You can buy cheesecloth at the kitchen section of most stores. Store the container in a cool, shaded place.

❁ Put small twigs in the container to give your caterpillar a place to attach its chrysalis. Feed your caterpillar fresh, clean leaves daily. Remember, caterpillars have huge appetites!

✿ Be a good housekeeper and clean the container daily. Put down new paper towels to prevent mold.

✿ When caterpillars are about to molt, they usually look dull in color and shrunken. Do not move them during this stage. Any disturbance will prevent molting.

✿ Once the caterpillar is full-grown, it will hang itself upside down from a twig. In one or two days, it will form a green- or gold-tinted chrysalis. This is the butterfly's rest period. Do not disturb or touch it.

✿ Soon you will see the Monarch's black and orange wings through the chrysalis. You will want to watch your butterfly closely now. It will emerge in about ten to fourteen days, once its wings have formed and hardened. (Other butterfly species can take up to nine months to emerge.)

Monarchs gather together in large groups before they migrate south.

❧ To feed your butterfly, you will need to make a mixture that is like its regular food, nectar. Mix together water and sugar (not honey). Soak a Q-tip in the sugar water and let your butterfly touch it with its legs. You also can pour the mixture onto a paper towel and place the butterfly on top of it.

Within a week, you will want to free your butterfly into the wild. It's important to allow the insect to find a mate. In this way, you are helping to continue the life cycle of butterflies.

The Magnificent Monarch Migration

The Monarch has one of the longest life spans of any butterfly species. Monarchs that are born in late summer can live between seven and nine months. A long life span allows them time to travel south.

Every winter, Monarchs fly thousands of miles to migrate (move to warmer areas). Tens of thousands of Monarchs fill the sky each year during the fall. As high as 3,000 feet (910 m) in the air, Monarchs sail over cities and mountains. They travel up to 200 miles (322 km) a day. Some Monarchs head to Florida, others to Costa Rica. Most of them land in Mexico, where entire trees, bushes, and fields disappear under a blanket of orange and black. Scientists believe that Monarchs have made this journey every year for millions of years, long before humans roamed the Earth.

5

Butterfly Gardening and Conservation

Butterfly gardening is a great way to watch butterflies up close and, at the same time, give something back to nature. When you plant a butterfly garden full of plants and flowers, you are helping to feed and grow all forms of wildlife. It also will make your yard a more enjoyable place for all creatures.

STARTING A BUTTERFLY GARDEN

The first step is to plant and grow flowers that are rich in a butterfly's favorite food, nectar. See page 35 for the types of plants on which butterflies like to feed. Make sure you grow plants that flower during different seasons. This way, butterflies can feed in your garden throughout the year.

Monarch butterflies are attracted to brightly colored flowers, such as marigolds.

Something else to remember when planting a butterfly garden is sunlight. Butterflies need sunlight to keep them warm, but the outside temperature also can become too hot for them. A good butterfly garden should provide both sunny places and shady places. In the shade, butterflies can cool off as they eat.

You also will want to grow the plants that caterpillars like to eat. This will encourage butterflies to lay their eggs in your garden.

WHAT TO PLANT

With a little research, you can find out which butterfly species live in your area. Then you can grow a variety of plants to attract different species of butterflies. If you have a lot of space, you can try planting a wild garden where native plants can grow. Native plants also will attract butterflies.

The following are some common, easy-to-grow plants that attract many butterfly species.

A Zebra Swallowtail feeds on the nectar of flowers.

- ❀ Bee balm
- ❀ Butterfly Bush
- ❀ Butterfly Weed (or other milkweeds)
- ❀ Hebe
- ❀ Lantana
- ❀ Lilac
- ❀ Marjoram
- ❀ Purple coneflowers
- ❀ Sage
- ❀ Sunflowers
- ❀ Zinnias

Butterflies are not only beautiful, they also help the environment.

Do not use insecticides or pesticides in your garden! These chemical products will kill butterflies and caterpillars. Instead, grow plants that naturally keep pests away, such as marigolds, sweet basil, lavender, and mint.

NATURE'S HELPERS

Butterflies are some of nature's most delicate creatures. And even though they are small, they play a big role in the environment. As bees do, butterflies help keep plant life growing by pollinating many different types of flowers. Certain caterpillars, such as those that become Harvester butterflies, eat harmful pests, including aphids.

ENVIRONMENTAL INDICATORS

Butterflies are sensitive to the smallest changes in the environment. It is because of this sensitivity that butterflies are known to scientists as indicators. Indicators are certain animal species

Butterfly Watchers

One of the most important butterfly watchers was a popular stage actor from San Francisco, California. In the late 1800s, Henry Edwards was known to be as passionate about butterfly collecting as he was about the art of acting. Edwards devoted much of his time to studying butterflies. He was the first to describe the Oregon Swallowtail, a native of the Pacific Northwest. In 1979, this butterfly was adopted as Oregon's official state insect.

that scientists can study to learn more about the condition of the natural world. So, if a particular breed of butterfly suddenly becomes extinct (no longer exists), or if it vanishes from a particular area, it is a sign that there is trouble in the environment.

ENDANGERED BUTTERFLIES

The U.S. Fish and Wildlife Service lists more than twenty species of butterflies as endangered. An endangered species is one that is in danger of becoming extinct. These butterfly species are endangered because of the loss of their habitat. A habitat is an area where an animal or insect naturally lives and grows.

Around the world, loss of habitat is the main reason why certain butterfly species are endangered. Many rare butterflies live in tropical rain forests, such as those in Mexico and New Guinea. As these rain forests are destroyed, so are the butterflies' habitats.

The Palos Verde Blue butterfly is an endangered species.

Another reason why particular butterfly species are endangered is because they are being collected and traded. They are sold to museums and private collectors around the world. There are stories of people collecting and smuggling thousands of endangered butterfly species across international borders.

WHAT YOU CAN DO

As a butterfly watcher, you can do your part by respecting the insect and the environment in which it lives. Try not to handle butterflies, especially their wings. Be sensitive to their habitat. Grow plants that provide food for butterflies. Contact your local wildlife or conservation office about ways you can help to protect butterfly species in your state.

EDUCATE YOURSELF

Butterfly watching takes practice. But with practice, you will become a better butterfly watcher. Over time, you will begin to learn more about different butterfly species. You also will become better at recognizing the places where you can look for butterflies. With practice, you will be able to identify different species of butterflies without needing to consult your guidebook. Who knows, someday you may even become a famous lepidopterist!

With practice, you will be able to identify butterfly species by sight.

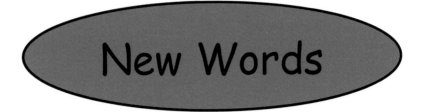

New Words

abdomen the part of an insect located below the thorax; the tail

antenna(e) one of two sensors on an insect's head

aphids a type of garden pest

camouflage coloring that helps a creature blend in with its environment

caterpillar the larva of a butterfly

chrysalis the resting stage of development when a caterpillar, enclosed in a hard, protective shell, turns into an adult

conservatory a place where nature is preserved, and animals and natural resources are protected

diurnal active during daylight

endangered a species that is in danger of no longer existing

forewings the front wings of a butterfly

hindwings the rear wings of a butterfly

indicators certain creatures that can be observed to learn more about the condition of the natural world

insecticide a chemical used to kill insects

larva the eating and growing stage of the butterfly; the caterpillar

lepidopterist a scientist who studies butterflies

mandibles jaws

migrate to move to a warmer area

molt the process by which a caterpillar sheds its skin

nectar the sugary fluid produced by the flowers of many plants; a butterfly's main source of food

nocturnal active at night

pesticide a chemical used to kill pests

pollinate to carry pollen from plant to plant

proboscis the mouth, or tongue, of a butterfly

pupa see chrysalis

scales tiny hairs on a butterfly's body

thorax the chest, or middle part, of an insect's body

wingspan the distance between the tips of an insect's wings

For Further Reading

Brimner, Gary Dave. *Butterflies & Moths*. Danbury, CT: Children's Press, 1999.

Hamilton, Kersten. *The Butterfly Book: A Kid's Guide to Attracting, Raising, and Keeping Butterflies*. Santa Fe: John Muir Publications, 1997.

Lasky, Kathryn and Christopher G. Knight. *Monarchs*. San Diego: Harcourt Brace & Company, 1993.

Norsgaard, Jaediker E. and John F. McGee. *Butterflies for Kids*. Minnetonka, MN: Creative Publishing International, Inc., 1996.

Taylor, Barbara. *Butterflies and Moths*. New York: DK Publishing, 1996.

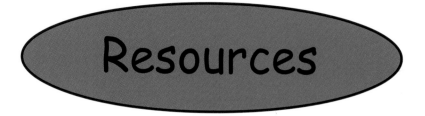

Resources

Butterflies, On the Wings of Freedom
http://library.thinkquest.org/27968/index.shtml
You can learn about how butterflies grow, how they protect themselves, and what they eat on this fascinating Web site.

Children's Butterfly Site
ww.mesc.usgs.gov/butterfly/Butterfly.html
The gallery of butterfly photos on this site has pictures of butterflies from different continents. The coloring page explains the life cycle of the butterfly and provides pictures that you can download and print.

The Butterfly Web Site
www.butterflywebsite.com
This site contains stories and information about butterflies. You can check out the chat room and photo gallery to learn more about different species of butterflies.

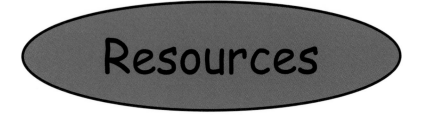

Resources

The Butterfly Zone
www.butterflies.com
This site contains all you need to know about starting a butterfly garden. It includes information on the types of butterflies around the world, and the kinds of plants that attract different butterflies.

Zoom Butterflies—All About Butterflies
www.EnchantedLearning.com/subjects/butterflies/allabout
This site provides information about butterflies, including their diet, habitat, and life cycle. It also contains tips on how to make your own butterfly garden.

Index

47

Index

About the Author

Ned Simonson is a freelance writer living in New York City.